The E

by Norman Stevens

Cover, ©Rolf W. Hapke/zefa/Corbis; p.3, ©Charles O. Cecil/Visuals Unlimited; p.4–5, ©TIM FITZHARRIS/Minden Pictures; p.6, ©age fotostock/SuperStock; p.7, p.10, ©Kevin Fleming/CORBIS; p.8-9, ©James J. Stachecki/Animals Animals; p.9, ©James Robinson/Animals Animals; p.11, ©PhotoDisc/PunchStock; p.12 (t) ©Rob & Ann Simpson/Visuals Unlimited, (b) ©John Pontier/Animals Animals, (c) U.S. Fish and Wildlife Service; p.13, ©Beth Davidow/Visuals Unlimited; p.14, ©Randy Wells/Getty Images.

Cartography, p.5, Joe LeMonnier

Printed in the United States of America

ISBN 10: 0-15-350498-6
ISBN 13: 978-0-15-350498-3

Ordering Options
ISBN 10: 0-15-350333-5 (Grade 3 Below-Level Collection)
ISBN 13: 978-0-15-350333-7 (Grade 3 Below-Level Collection)
ISBN 10: 0-15-357485-2 (package of 5)
ISBN 13: 978-0-15-357485-6 (package of 5)

1 2 3 4 5 6 7 8 9 10 179 12 11 10 09 08 07 06

The Everglades in Florida is a place made up of water and marsh grasses. It is the largest wild place in the warm region of the United States. The Everglades shelters many kinds of plants and animals. Alligators, bobcats, and deer all live there.

Many think the Everglades is a big swamp. That is not true. Water does not move in a swamp. Water in the Everglades flows from Lake Okeechobee toward the sea. Lake Okeechobee is shallow. When heavy rains fall, the water overflows.

The water drifts out over the land. At the center of the Everglades, the water is a few feet deep. In some places it is only six-inches deep. Many types of plants can grow here. That is why the Everglades is sometimes called a "river of grass."

The wet season here lasts from May to November. A lot of rain falls. The water rises. More plants grow. Animals wander the Everglades in search of a place to live. Then they have their babies and raise them.

The dry season lasts from December to April, but the Everglades is never really dry. The water goes down, so parts of the land show. Animals then can find food more easily.

Some people call alligators "keepers of the Everglades." During the dry season, alligators dig holes to keep wet. These "gator holes" hold water. Other animals, such as fish, snakes, and turtles use these "gator holes" to get the water that they need during the dry season.

Alligator mothers lay about thirty eggs. They take care of their babies for two years. This is important. Many other animals try to eat baby alligators. A young alligator can grow a foot (.30m) a year if it gets enough food.

Today, the Everglades is only half the size it was. People have moved into the marshland. They changed the habitat by making the water drain in a different direction to dry out parts of the land. After that, they built houses there. Destroying a natural habitat hurts plants and animals.

Everglades National Park protects a small part of the Everglades, but what happens in the rest of the Everglades can affect the plants and animals in the park.

Today, some plants and animals are in trouble. Wading birds, such as the wood stork, are becoming scarce because they need wild places where they can nest and find food.

The future also looks dim for many other plants and animals. Several kinds of turtles, birds, and mice are dying out. The Florida panther, a large wild cat, may soon be gone. Rare plants, flowers, and butterflies are disappearing.

Many people are working to save the Everglades. People study the animals living there to see what they need. Workers hope to restore the waterways. It is not an easy job.

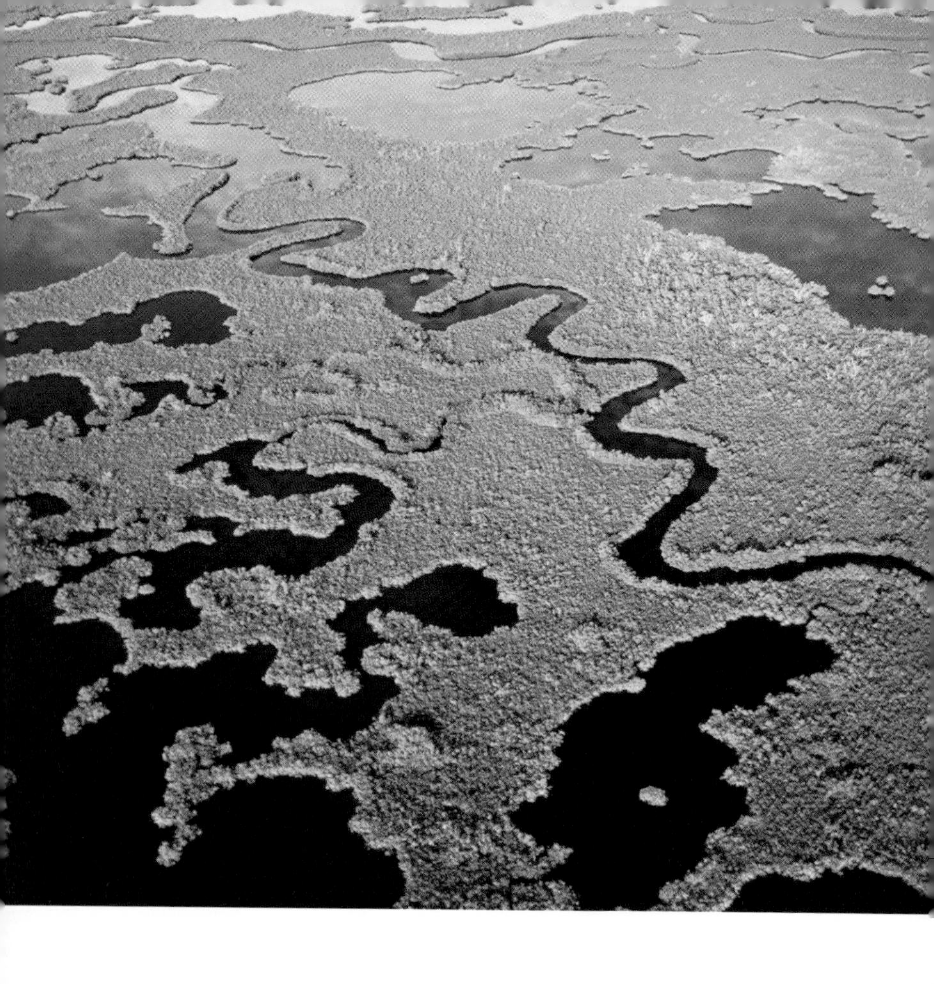

It will take time to permanently save the Everglades. The absence of the Everglades would be bad for our world in many ways. It is a rich, green part of our planet. It is home to many plants and animals.

Think Critically

1. What happened to some of the plants and animals after more people started to move to the marshlands?
2. What happens in the wet season between May and November?
3. How do alligators help the Everglades during the dry season?
4. Why are many animals in the Everglades in danger?
5. Why do some people call the Everglades a "river of grass"?

Science

Animals of the Everglades Look at some photographs of Everglades animals. Then draw your own pictures of them. Write captions for your pictures.

School-Home Connection Alligators are reptiles. Ask family members to name other reptiles. Make a list. Look up reptiles on the Internet or in a book, if necessary.

Word Count: 511